UNOFFICIAL
GUIDES
JUNIOR

Starter Guide to
Animal Crossing

T0002289

by Josh Gregory

CHERRY LAKE PRESS
Ann Arbor, Michigan

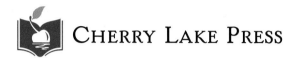

Cherry Lake Press

Published in the United States of America by Cherry Lake Publishing
Ann Arbor, Michigan
www.cherrylakepublishing.com

Reading Adviser: Beth Walker Gambro, MS, Ed., Reading Consultant, Yorkville, IL

Photo Credits: Images by Josh Gregory

Copyright © 2024 by Cherry Lake Publishing Group

Cherry Lake Press is an imprint of Cherry Lake Publishing Group.

Library of Congress Cataloging-in-Publication Data has been filed and is available at catalog.loc.gov

Printed in the United States of America by
Corporate Graphics

Note from the Publisher: Websites change regularly, and their future contents are outside of our control. Supervise children when conducting any recommended online searches for extended learning opportunities

Contents

A Fun World

Canberra

Hey! I'm trying to be more neighborly and get to know folks better, and I wanna know about you. That cool?

In *Animal Crossing*, there's no one to compete with or a way to win or lose.

Picture an island paradise. In this world, there are no deadlines or threats. You can make friends with cute animals. You can also design your own house—as well as the whole island. How do you get there? All you need to do is play *Animal Crossing*!

How to Play

Interested in trying *Animal Crossing* for yourself? Play it on a Nintendo Switch.

Starting the Game

Get to know Timmy and Tommy and hundreds of different animal characters in *Animal Crossing*.

When you first play *Animal Crossing*, you'll find yourself in Nook Inc. There, you'll meet Timmy and Tommy Nook. They will offer you a "getaway package." It will take you to an island paradise. This package is just the start of your journey. Then you can create your character!

Your **Character**

Skin Tone

Confirm.

B Cancel   A Select

Your character in *Animal Crossing* can look
like you—or not! The choice is yours.

You can choose the way your character looks. Select different hairstyles and skin colors. Don't worry! You can always change your **appearance** later in the game. You'll also be able to unlock new styles as you play.

Island Time

Characters in *Animal Crossing* experience the same holidays as people in real life!

Next, tell Timmy and Tommy if you live in the Northern or Southern **Hemisphere**. In *Animal Crossing*, time passes and seasons change—just like they do in real life. If you play at night, it will be nighttime in the game. If you play during winter, it will be winter.

Your Island's Layout

Each island layout includes lots of places to go fishing.

The next step is picking your island's layout. Timmy and Tommy will show you some options. These are **random**. So every player will get something different. However, all the islands have rivers and beaches. Now it's time to fly to your island home!

Sleep Function

If you need to take a break from playing *Animal Crossing*, you can use the Switch's sleep function. If you plan to play something else, be sure to save your progress and quit through the in-game menu!

Settling In

Later in the game, Tom Nook's home becomes a place called the Resident Services building.

After you land on your island, you will head to the **plaza**. The plaza is an important meeting place. There you will meet Tom. He is the owner of Nook Inc. Tom will give you goals to work toward. Next, you will choose a spot for your tent. Choose it carefully! It will become the site for your house.

Creating a Home

5:00 PM

Nook Miles+

B Put Away A Select

Another type of money is called Nook Miles. To earn them, you must complete special tasks on your NookPhone.

A big part of the game is building your home. You'll also create your neighbors' homes! Soon, Tom Nook will ask you to gather supplies. The supplies are for a welcome party in the plaza. Then Tom will give you a cot to sleep on. After you rest, he'll give you a NookPhone to use. Finally, Tom will ask you to pay for your trip.

Money Called Bells

Money in Animal Crossing is called Bells. One way to make money is to collect fruit, seashells, and bugs. Then you can sell them to Timmy and Tommy for Bells.

Supplies

Ladder

X Remove/Register   B Cancel   A Hold

You can unlock an item called the tool ring. It lets you pick different tools by pressing the up arrow button.

You can take as long as you want to pay Tom. Fill your time by finding more supplies, such as seashells. Then you can **craft** these items into tools. The tools may be a fishing pole or a shovel. Use the tools to catch fish and find **fossils**.

Critterpedia

You can also catch wildlife. The Critterpedia app logs which wildlife you have captured in the game.

What's Next?

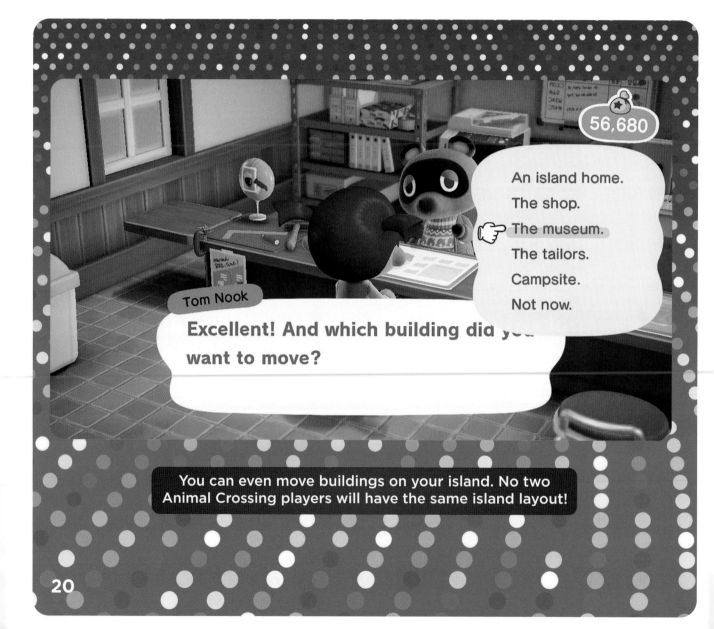

56,680

An island home.
The shop.
☞ The museum.
The tailors.
Campsite.
Not now.

Tom Nook

Excellent! And which building did you want to move?

You can even move buildings on your island. No two Animal Crossing players will have the same island layout!

Once you get far enough into *Animal Crossing*, you can change your island. You can move waterways, add paths, and much more. However, you'll need a lot of Bells to do this! So, feel free to **experiment**. If you need some ideas, see what other players have done. You can do a lot with a little imagination!

GLOSSARY

appearance (up-PEER-uhns) the way someone or something looks

craft (KRAFT) to make or build something

experiment (ek-SPER-uh-ment) to try out something new

fossils (FAH-suhlz) the remains or impressions of living things from the distant past

hemisphere (HEM-uh-sfeer) half of the planet

plaza (PLAH-zuh) a public space often located in the central area of a town

random (RAN-duhm) chosen without a conscious decision

FIND OUT MORE

BOOKS

Cunningham, Kevin. *Video Game Designer*. Ann Arbor, MI: Cherry Lake Publishing, 2016.

Loh-Hagan, Virginia. *Video Games*. Ann Arbor, MI: Cherry Lake Publishing, 2021.

Powell, Marie. *Asking Questions About Video Games*. Ann Arbor, MI: Cherry Lake Publishing, 2016.

WEBSITES

With an adult, learn more online with these suggested searches:

Animal Crossing Wiki
This fan-created site is packed with info about every detail of the *Animal Crossing* games.

Island News—Animal Crossing: New Horizons
Keep up to date with the latest official news updates about *Animal Crossing*.

INDEX

ABOUT THE AUTHOR

Josh Gregory is the author of more than 200 books for kids. He has written about everything from animals to technology to history. A graduate of the University of Missouri–Columbia, he currently lives in Chicago, Illinois.